LETTERS TO

On Equality

I Wish
Laura Bates

AND

The Men You'll Meet
Owen Sheers

HAY FESTIVAL PRESS

2018

Published May 2018 by

Hay Festival Press
The Drill Hall
25 Lion Street
Hay-on-Wye HR3 5AD
United Kingdom

www.hayfestival.org

ISBN 978-1-9996015-0-8

Typeset by Timothy Symons
Printed by Impact Print, Hereford

Hay Festival is committed to a sustainable future for our
business, our readers and our planet. This book is made of
Forest Stewardship Council certified paper.

CONTENTS

Introduction

Laura Bates, the founder of the Everyday Sexism Project, has been inspiring women and men for many years, speaking in schools, colleges and at festivals. At Hay Festival last year, to celebrate our 30th anniversary, which coincided with the 500th anniversary of Martin Luther's Theses, we commissioned 30 Reformations from our international speakers. Owen Sheers, inspired by Laura Bates to look at the conversations we need to have with boys and men, reformed Masculinity. His tender, challenging poem addressed to his daughters, *The Men You'll Meet*, was delivered to live audiences at Hay Festival. This year we have commissioned Laura Bates to write her own letter to future generations, *I Wish*. Together these Letters produce a book rich in insight about the work needed to create a gender-equal society, and together make a hard and hopeful book.

This book is for adults and young people exploring all the issues around equality and gender that face societies everywhere. We hope that it will provoke discussion and engagement, and that it will sit alongside some of the further recommended reading both authors have suggested here.

If you are a teacher, there are suggested lesson plans to use alongside this book, written by The National Literacy Trust and available from our website hayfestival.org.

I Wish

Laura Bates

I wish you a world where you're safe and whole
Where your sex is more than a rigid mask
I wish you a world with every choice
Is that really still too much to ask?

I WISH you a world where children are equal. Where your tiny baby clothes won't imprint you with the rigid expectation of a 'future superhero' or 'pretty princess' before you even know what the words mean. Where blue boys' onesies don't predict a future president while the purple girls' version proclaims: 'I hate my thighs'. Ages 0–3 months.

I wish you televisions without yoghurt adverts telling you chubby boys are strong like daddy and roly-poly girls wear heels like mummy. A world where picking up a stethoscope in a toddler playgroup doesn't earn you the immediate, cooing label of doctor or nurse from a well-meaning nearby adult. Both such brilliant careers. Ones you should have the right to choose for yourself.

I wish you a world where you don't arrive in the toy store, bright with excitement and saved-up pocket money, to rush towards the toy kitchen or the science kit you've dreamed of, only to falter, and then stop short. Because the aisle is blue, or pink. The toy you coveted labelled 'for girls' or 'for boys'. Not for you.

I wish you a world where a boy picking up a dolly doesn't cause a sharp intake of breath.

I wish you a childhood where girls don't receive 20% less pocket money than their brothers. Where children all do the same amount of chores. Where boys aren't taught that the burden of financial responsibility is theirs from childhood because parents are more likely to give them money and more likely to buy things for their sisters. Where girls don't learn that it's their job to clear the table and make the beds while their brothers play outside.

I wish you a world where you will never hear that 'boys don't cry'.

I wish you children's parties where your dressing-up choices are as varied and unique as you and all your friends. Where girls can be pirates and boys can bake cakes. Where the superhero books we read at bedtime don't feature passive princesses rescued by strong silent knights over and over again. Where we visit the shoe shop and you pick the colours you like instead of being told 'those aren't for you'. Where dinosaurs and sparkles aren't off limits to anyone. Where your character, not your sex, decides your options. Boys' clothes that don't stop you from enjoying fluffy pink embellishment that you can run your fingers through and giggle. A range for girls that isn't so flimsy and impractical it stops you climbing trees.

I wish you pockets. Pockets for all!

I wish you supermarkets where the magazines you see as you whizz round in the little plastic seat in the front of the trolley don't send you messages about what you can and can't do. Don't show you diet, cooking and celebrity weeklies under a heading of 'Women's Magazines' while science, economy, geography and politics are labelled 'Men's'.

I wish you a world where 'like a girl' is a compliment, instead of an insult.

I want your childish exploration of who you are not to result in rigid categorisation. No future roles imposed on you while you're still trying on who you might yet become. Your youthful exuberance shouldn't see girls labelled 'bossy' and sensitivity shouldn't be weaponised against boys and your childhood play should remain fluid instead of hardening rigidly into someone else's decisions about who you are.

I wish you books about female scientists and explorers and engineers, where children's book characters are brave and vulnerable and emotional, regardless of their gender. I want you to read books of all kinds, and not to see the boys' title 'how to be clever' next to the girls' equivalent 'how to be gorgeous'. I wish you children's magazines that don't offer girls as young as seven tips on getting rid of cellulite, applying enough make-up and snaring the perfect man. I wish you electronic devices that don't contain plastic surgery apps targeted at little girls.

I wish these weren't real examples.

I wish you a world where boys aren't bullied for taking dance or drama, and the A-level physics classrooms at over half of all State schools aren't empty of girls. Where your ambitions aren't dictated or stunted by your gender, where primary school children don't think doctors are men and nurses are women and 'girls can't be airline pilots because you have to be really good at maths and women make too many mistakes'. I wish you diverse role models. I wish you a world where watching the sickening abuse of women in the public eye doesn't put you off ever considering a career in journalism or politics.

I want you to believe you can be anything you want to be.

I wish you classrooms where you aren't fearful for your safety, where a third of teenage girls aren't sexually assaulted at school, where boys don't 'rate' you out of 10 as you walk in and teachers don't reply 'boys will be boys' when you are sexually harassed. I wish more than anything that you won't become accustomed to accepting sexual harassment as 'normal'. I wish you streets where men don't shout about your developing bodies in words so explicit you don't even know what they mean. I want you to go to school in your uniform without someone stroking your legs or rubbing up against you with an erection as you try to ride the bus.

I wish you a world where these experiences aren't met with shrugs and eye rolls and questions such as 'What were you wearing?' and 'Did you lead him on?' Where we don't call it 'groping' or 'unwanted sexual touching'. Where we're explicit about sexual assault. Where young women don't feel they can never report what's illegal because, really, where would they begin? I wish you a world where sexual abuse isn't normal.

I wish you school dress codes that don't sexualise and sensationalise girls' knees and collarbones and shoulders and teach you that boys can't control their wandering attention and male teachers shouldn't be subjected to unfair 'temptation'. I want you to wear what you want, without adults forcing objectification onto your developing body parts before you have become conscious of them yourself. I wish you schools where boys can wear skirts and have long hair and the flash of an underage bra strap isn't considered a deliberate provocation. Where black girls' natural hair isn't described as a 'distraction' and trans pupils aren't forced to choose between conforming to a rigid gender binary or being expelled.

I wish you teenage years where nude photographs of underage girls aren't precious currency, where they aren't extracted through coercion and wheedling and taunts. Where there is a choice for girls beyond 'slut' or 'frigid' and boys aren't pressured to breaking point to use pictures to prove they are 'lads'.

I wish for 'prude' and 'slag' not to be your only options.

I wish you a world where you're not blamed for what happens to you. Where schools don't brush sexual assault under the carpet to protect their reputations and sexual harassment is discussed, not hushed up. I wish for a world where you have open, supportive conversations at school about consent and healthy relationships. Is that really too much to ask?

I want you to know that a boyfriend can rape his girlfriend.

I don't want any child ever again to tell me 'but you have to have sex with him if he's your boyfriend. You don't have any choice'. I wish you a world where a rapist isn't just a stranger in a dark alleyway. Where newspapers and jurors and members of the public blame perpetrators of sexual violence instead of their victims. Where victims feel able to report what has happened to them. Where trials end in convictions instead of the vilification of survivors.

I wish you a world where women are safe.

I wish you newspapers where 84% of the front-page stories you read aren't just about men, and more than a quarter of front-page news articles are written by women. A media where women in the public eye are presented as complex, talented human beings instead of sex objects.

I hope you will see and hear women.

I want women to represent more than 15% of the statues you wonder at as you stroll through UK cities, and I want more than two to be of a named, black woman. I want you to see paintings women have painted hanging in art galleries instead of just pictures of naked women painted beautifully by men. I want you to hear women's voices on screens, where more than 28% of Hollywood speaking parts are female, where over half of teenage girls on screen aren't sexualised and women don't take their clothes off in the movies three times more often than men.

I want you to see women as the story instead of the illustration.

I wish you television screens that show as much women's sport as men's. I want you to watch sport without seeing men compete while women decorate. I wish you a world where boys who don't like sports aren't devalued and dismissed and girls who want to do them aren't cowed by the fear they'll seem unattractive, when only one tenth of teenage girls are doing enough sport to benefit their health.

Where the Women's World Cup is called the World Cup.

I wish you a workplace that doesn't begin with a pay gap, where you don't watch men discouraged from taking paternity leave or denied it altogether while women drop away at senior management level as over 50,000 lose their jobs each year through maternity discrimination. Where 12 million women don't have experiences of workplace sexual harassment to share but, if they do, where their shared pain isn't dismissed as a 'witch hunt' against men. Where women feel able to report workplace sexual harassment, and policies protect them from harm instead of shielding companies from 'reputational damage'.

I wish you a world where reporting abuse doesn't mean coming into contact with justice systems suffused with misogynistic and racist prejudice.

Where you can say out loud what has happened to you.

I wish you bodies that are protected instead of policed. An adolescence where consent isn't shrouded in silence and sex in shameful secrecy. Where we teach children from reception to respect one another's bodies and boundaries, in exactly the same way we would teach a young child that it isn't OK to hit.

I wish that wasn't seen as a shockingly progressive concept.

I wish you a diet of everything you want, where Kinder eggs aren't blue and pink and happy meal toys aren't split down the middle and girls are never told they've taken too much or ought to watch their weight. I wish for boys to eat because food is delicious, not because they're told they have to grow up big and strong.

I hope you never hear that nothing tastes as good as skinny feels.

I wish you a world where women are valued by more than the gap between their thighs. Where girls of five aren't worried about the size and shape of their bodies and a quarter of seven-year-old girls haven't dieted to lose weight. Where weight-loss isn't a preoccupation that devastates and swallows up the lives and headspace of women.

I wish for you never to learn the phrase 'thunder thighs'.

I wish you an internet where you can go online without receiving rape threats. I wish for you never to have to hold your keys between your fingers as you walk home at night. I wish for you never to be told you should take precautions to protect yourself from violence. I wish you a world where we tackle the violence instead.

I wish you a world where we join the dots. Where the murder of a woman and her children by her husband isn't reported over and over again on the nightly news, but always described as an 'isolated incident'. Where we're allowed to challenge media sexism and street harassment and all the other insidious, 'low-level' forms of discrimination without being called nitpickers, because we can see how they connect to the more serious forms of abuse. Because we consider it unacceptable for girls and women to experience 'low-level' abuse as well. Because we come to think of women as human beings.

I wish for women to be treated like human beings.

I wish you women's services that are funded instead of cut smaller and smaller until they fall away altogether. Where it's not considered a better investment to spend millions of pounds on a nuclear deterrent for a hypothetical future threat than a fraction of the cost on life-saving services for the two women a week who are killed by a current or former partner.

I wish you a world where two women a week are not killed by a current or former partner.

Where hundreds of women aren't turned away from refuges daily. Where specialist services for BAME women receive the support they deserve instead of disappearing to be replaced by generic organisations without the same long-cultivated expertise. Where raped women don't have to 'prove' the conception was non-consensual to access benefits for extra children. Where refugee women are not detained indefinitely, their stories of sexual violence disbelieved. Where women have the right to access safe, comprehensive reproductive healthcare without intimidation or shame.

I wish you a world where women are in control of their own bodies.

I wish you a society where intervention is normal. Where nobody walks past on the other side of the street. Where being sexually assaulted on public transport is met with gasps and outrage and action instead of silence and surreptitious sideways glances. Where workplace sexual harassment doesn't flourish because of 'good' men's silence. Where nobody turns a blind eye to misogyny in meetings. Where people step in when they see abuse on the street. Where campuses and classrooms and supermarkets and cinemas are safer because of our shared vigilance and action. Where shock and shame are attached to staying silent instead of stepping in. Where we take a collective responsibility for our shared spaces. Where we say 'Not on our watch'. Where the standard we walk past is the standard we accept. Where men and boys of all ages engage their peers in conversation and challenge each other. Where it's not good enough not to be part of the problem unless you are part of the solution too.

Nobody can do everything. But I wish that everybody would do something.

I wish you a world where it's not controversial to talk about women's rights. Where feminism is not a dirty word. Where we don't have to fight just to be heard before we can even begin to think about the problem. A world where broadcasters don't consider rape and assault fodder for 'feisty debate'. Where a girl who starts a school feminist society doesn't find herself attacked and bullied. Where women who speak out are not branded troublemakers or harpies or ball-breakers. Where politicians who put their heads above the parapet aren't shot down with streams of abuse.

I wish you a world where I never have to talk to you about all this, because we've fixed it.

And how will we fix it?

What shall we tell our daughters? They ask me, over and over again. What shall we tell our daughters to fix this? Tell us what to tell our daughters.

But why aren't we telling our sons? Don't they need help and support and love and instructions as well? Don't they have a role to play in creating this brave new world? Aren't they as bewildered and confused by the bombardment of gender roles and expectations and online porn? Their place is in this conversation too, not outside playing football while the girls are taught about periods and holding a pill between their knees to keep themselves from being raped.

Does that mean all boys are rapists? Of course it doesn't. But all boys are likely to know one. Does it mean all girls will be raped? No. But all girls are likely to know somebody who is.

Why tell our daughters to move in packs and wear longer skirts and stick to well-lit streets? Why teach them about crossing the road and moving to a crowded place and, if all else fails, shouting FIRE because people are more likely to respond to that than RAPE?

Why teach them all this when we know that it makes no difference?

Why teach our daughters to keep themselves safe from shadowy strangers when the man most likely to attack them is their husband or their colleague, their boyfriend or their housemate? Why tell them to avoid dark streets blind drunk at 2 o'clock in the morning in a short skirt when they're safer there than at home in bed in their own pyjamas? When women of all ages are raped all over the world in all types of clothing at all times of day. Is it because we can't face the truth?

The truth is, the only thing rape victims have in common is that they came into contact with a rapist.

Perhaps we could start there.

'What shall we teach our daughters?' They ask, and I say: 'Let's not teach them anything'. Unless it is this. Unless it is to be loud and free and take up space and never to apologise. Unless it is to be bold and brave and unashamed and not to let the world pack you up into smaller and smaller boxes performing its bullshit rules and gender stereotypes that reduce and diminish and close you in. Unless it is to be free to be whoever you are and play with whatever toy you like and pursue whatever hobbies you like and consider every career and fuck their beauty standards and never cast your eyes down the way women do in the movies and always, always, when someone tells you 'It's the way things are', ask: 'WHY?'

To wear what you want and go where you like and flourish in your freedom and speak out with confidence and challenge authority and use public space and shriek, yes, shriek, and scream, and shout out loud when they're sexist.

Unless it's to let your body grow into the shape it naturally wants and eat when you're hungry and stop when you're full and speak when you have an idea and tell them when they're wrong and be just exactly, exactly who you are.

Tell us what to teach our daughters, they ask, and I refuse. I won't. I will not teach you how to jump higher and higher over the hurdles life puts in front of you. But I will fight like a tiger to move the hurdles out of your way.

Imagine a world where none of this is normal. Where an all-male panel looks strange and uneven. Where posters telling women how to avoid rape are laughable. Where the notion of a chemistry set being just for boys is utterly bizarre.

Imagine a world where unequal parliaments are strange, where businesses run just by men are abnormal, where sexual violence is an aberration instead of the wallpaper.

Where we see the strangeness and the futility and the limitations of it all. Where we look back and marvel at how we went on like this for so long. Where we laugh at how silly it all was.

Imagine a world where all this is a thing of the past.

I wish you that world.

Laura Bates is the founder of the Everyday Sexism Project, an ever-increasing collection of over 100,000 testimonies of gender inequality. The project has expanded into over 20 countries worldwide and become internationally renowned, featuring in media from the *New York Times* to the *Times of India*.

Laura writes regularly for the *Guardian*, *New York Times* and others. She was the recipient of the Georgina Henry Award at the 2015 British Press Awards. Her first book, *Everyday Sexism*, was shortlisted for Waterstones Book of the Year and the Political Book Awards Polemic of the Year. Her second book, the *Sunday Times* bestseller *Girl Up*, was published in 2016 and her latest, *Misogynation*, in 2018.

Laura works closely with politicians, schools and universities worldwide, as well as bodies from the United Nations to the Council of Europe to combat gender inequality. She is also a contributor for Women Under Siege, a New York-based organisation working against the use of rape as a tool of war in conflict zones, and she is Patron of Somerset and Avon Rape and Sexual Abuse Support, part of the Rape Crisis network.

Laura was awarded a British Empire Medal in The Queen's Birthday Honours List in 2015. She has been named a Woman of the Year by *The Sunday Times* and *Cosmopolitan* and *Red* magazines, and was named ninth on the BBC Radio 4 Woman's Hour Power List 2014. That same year she received the Internet and Society Award from the Oxford Internet Institute alongside Tim Berners-Lee.

The Men You'll Meet

Owen Sheers

So, MY DAUGHTERS, one recently born,
the other still in the womb,
why is it, when asked what I'd like to reform,
my first thought was to address that reform to you?

Well, for me to reform means the future;
how we might mould it with imagination
into a better shape for all –
although I must admit, since I became your father,
it's become more specific – for you, my children,
my two girls who will grow into women.

And maybe that's why, when I cast a reforming eye
about our world, our lives,
viewing it through *your* bodies, your minds,
I kept seeing, at the root of so many of the ills that threaten you –
injustice, oppression, pollution and violence
– people like me, men.

I looked harder, and listened too –
put my ear to how we are, what we do,
tried to discern the undercurrents of our nurture,
the inherited habits and behaviours
which day by day it's so easy to forget are there.

And when I did, I heard others who'd seen the same,
and who were already having this conversation
of cause and concern about what we teach and learn
when it comes to ideas of what is 'to be a man'.

But I also saw this talk was, in the scheme of things, new,
still forming, a recent debate despite the age of the issue,
and its spread about our globe.
Which at first seemed odd – I mean the discussion about
what women might be, could be,
has been running for generations.
For decades women have been embracing change,
in themselves and society, as a path towards a fairer future.
As a sex and a gender they've looked *forward*, see?
And in doing so unlocked the parts of themselves
kept from them by society.
But men, well, we've hardly been doing the same.
But then isn't that always the way?
Attention is paid most by those paying the highest price,
and for men, living in our systems of patriarchal domination,
well, this has rarely, if ever, been them.

The white western male, and his equivalent in other cultures,
have made their worlds to fit them,
so they might reap its rewards most easily.
What are considered masculine traits
are more highly prized, advantages of life more accessible,
their assumed superiority unquestioned in plain sight,
so hey, why talk about what might be wrong or unhealthy
about masculinity –
if it ain't broke, don't fix it, right?

But maybe that's why those conversations I heard
when I put my ear to how we are,
about men and who we might be, *have* finally begun.
Because our traditional ideas of being a man are just that,
broken – outdated, unhelpful and harmful –
and not just to women and the poor,
but to everyone, including, I'd say, the majority of men.

Which is why I hope I'd be standing here now,
saying the same, if I didn't have daughters, but sons.
Because regardless of sex we need to talk, we really do, for once,
about what *men* might become –
take a lead from feminism and imagine what might they be,
and how might we, as a species, come, some day,
to equate a more positive charge with masculinity?

So, as you can see, what began as a pretty selfish view,
how to make the world better for my children, you,
and therefore for me, has grown somewhat,
to encompass the world, just, it has to be said,
as a certain variety of traditional, rouge, brittle, toxic,
call it what you will, masculinity has.

But if we're going to make progress, make no mistake,
both are going to have be addressed at once –
the intimate and the universal, the personal and the global –
how men are one-to-one, with each other and with women and
children,
but also how the idea of a man sits across our cultures, religions,
nations.

Because neither can happen alone. The personal informs the
political, the domestic the public, and vice versa –
a spiral of influence that tightens over time.
So it's *that* spiral we need to slow, unwind –
the way what we teach about gender becomes who we are,
until it feels like nature, the normal –
when really, mostly, it's not. It's nurture.

Which is why this tightening spiral can be our solution too –
What did Larkin say? 'Man hands on misery to man,
it deepens like an ocean shelf'?
Well, yes, but an ocean shelf slopes the other way too,
and we have to believe that instead of a deepening,
a shallowing of inherited pain is also in our power,
that what we pass on is what we become,
for good as well as bad,
otherwise how else is progress made?

So that's my stall, my daughters. The dominant perceptions
of masculinity, across the globe and cultures, is harming us all.
Men, women, girls, boys, humans, animals, flora and fauna.
But until recently, this hasn't been addressed. Why?
Because those same patriarchal ideas inform the systems
we live in until those perceptions aren't seen as choices at all,
but just how things are –
like the air, or the tides, or the shedding of leaves from a tree.

But to let that be? In the face of the evidence I've seen?
Well, that doesn't seem fair, or wise, or good enough to me.

*

Before I continue, let's get some things clear –
what I am, and am not talking about here.

Firstly, I know there are many kinds of men, and most, I hope
want to be good. And there is a degree of nuance in our being –
gay, straight, somewhere in-between, the geek, the muso,
the sportsman, the stay-at-home dad. But in general,
across the world, the 'rules' of being a man still, well, rule.
As a recent Samaritans report has put it,
men still compare themselves, when it comes to masculinity,
to a 'gold standard' which prizes, above all, power, control,
invincibility. So much of their being is taken up
with trying to prove their value and worth, not through
being who they are, but through what they do.
We expect boys to be boisterous rather than bookish,
fathers to be earners more than carers,
and for boys and men to be less attuned, emotionally,
than girls or women.

Which brings me to sex and gender, which,
and it's so important to hammer this home,
aren't the same thing at all.
Sex, you see, is about the chromosome. Biological fact.
You both have XX, while boys have XY,
and along with those pairs,
you more oestrogen, they, testosterone.
Because of this, our hardware, as many will jump to tell you,
isn't wired exactly the same, and I see how that could be true,
I really do.

Owen Sheers

I have a punch bag hanging in our barn.
Sometimes, when frustrated, angry,
I like to hit it, again and again. And then, I feel better.
Your mother, however, doesn't need to do the same.
If she's having those emotions she'll go somewhere quiet, alone,
or speak to her own mother on the phone.

All that said, at the same time, I know many women out there
who'd rather ease their frustration by hitting the bag,
and many men who'd do the same by going somewhere quiet,
alone, like your mum.
And this is what the surveys, the studies now show –
that in infant males and females, there's much more overlap than
difference,
that yes, those chromosomes govern us to a certain extent,
but that extent is more limited than we like to think,
and so no reason to justify unfair treatment,
or to cut down on choices for one group or another,
just because slightly more men hit the bag,
and slightly more women want to talk to their mother.

Because whatever our 'hardware', it's our software that runs us
and that, well that isn't written by genes but experience,
by example, in the pressures, both overt and subtle,
that tell us, from early in the cradle,
what it is to be not male or female, but a man or a woman.

Gender, you see, by definition, is a myth-made beast –
created upon a sketch of biological difference, yes,

but then fleshed out and given movement, action
with the stories, habits and often prejudice
that most benefits those holding the reins and the power.

To put it simply, sex, a biological category, is what we are,
and gender, a cultural category, is what we feel, think or are told
a man or woman should be –
what are the attributes of masculine or feminine,
what the expectations, behaviour, duties, rights and roles.

Chromosomes don't change, but thoughts and feelings do,
which means that ideas and perceptions of gender can too,
and often have.
Not long ago, for your great, great, great grandmother,
having a womb meant she couldn't vote, take part in politics
or expect to ever do the same jobs as a man.
Now, both of you, exactly the same kind of biological female,
aren't the same kind of woman – because you can.
The playing field is still far from level,
and God knows there's loads more to be done,
but in terms of imagining themselves
out of culture's constraining version of their gender,
then there's no doubt, it's men nil and women one.

Although of course, that's another problem –
that 'versus' trap into which I've just fallen.
The way in which, from early on, boys and girls
are routinely viewed in opposition: troublesome *v* compliant,
active *v* passive, loud *v* quiet.

Of course, masculinity's been fluid too,
flexing over the ages and time – 200 years ago
the power suit was a wig, tights and high heels,
while for the Spartans to be a 'real man'
meant sleeping with one was part of the deal.
But since the agricultural revolution, well,
there's been barely any change.
Perhaps in parenting we've made the greatest strides
(although nowhere near enough again),
but the baseline of what it means to be a man,
that's pretty much remained the same:

aggression, competitive, a provider who's protective,
emotionally – past the age of three, distant/reticent at best,
illiterate at worst – strong, brave and hard.
A father but not a carer. A hunter in modern dress,
bringing home the bacon, the higher wage, a human of rational
certainty. Powerful, an accumulator of wealth, tribal of instinct,
but stoically independent, if he needs to be.

American social scientists, in the 70s,
came up with four 'rules' of western masculinity –
'No sissy stuff', be 'a big wheel', a 'sturdy oak'
and 'give 'em hell'.
Now, five decades on, for most of the globe,
these markers haven't moved. Which is pretty crap,
I mean, I don't want the men you'll meet
to be restricted by these rules, I want them
to be informed by and have more options than that.

In fighting against discrimination over the same five decades
women have managed to move into more traditionally 'male'
roles,
which, let me stress, has been only for the good.
And the pressure for that movement is being kept up,
as it should – encouraging girls to study STEM, play rugby,
aim for the boardroom, the Oval Office, the director's chair,
the moon –
to *question* what society has told them makes a woman.

But where's the equivalent movement for boys?
The encouragement to broaden the bandwidth of what it means
to be a man?
To study the arts, be a full-time father, to value communication
over anger?
There are groups, attempts on a local scale, but on a global,
it isn't there
and as a result the options of what being a girl can mean
are much broader than those for a boy,
firstly because of feminism,
but also, it has to be said, because society still values the 'manly'
attributes the girls acquire over the feminine trait instead.

For those who question that, ask them this,
a scenario courtesy of Grayson Perry and his book
The Descent of Man.
A six-year-old girl, cropped hair, walks down the street wearing
jeans, waving a sword or a gun.
What do you think? Tomboy, right? A little girl, having fun.
A six-year-old boy walks just behind, long hair, wearing a skirt,
waving a wand.

What do you think? A sissy? A victim? I mean,
don't his parents worry how they'll all have it in for him?

So who's promoting this narrow definition of man? Well,
just about everyone. Advertising, toy shops, fathers, brothers,
films, games, our language, the internet, schools, sisters,
mothers.
'Boys will be boys' – when do we say that? Not when they've
solved a problem,
or painted a picture or helped someone.
More likely when they've been too rough,
misbehaved or maybe, even, cut back on their reading?
Because it's easier that way isn't it?
To give in to the idea that gender is fixed,
so all we can do is roll over and accept it?

At which point you may ask, why not?
You've been banging on about this problem of men, Dad,
but what exactly is it?
(At which point can I highlight we're calling it just that –
a problem,
an issue, not a crisis, as the papers often like it.
To say as such, to quote once again from Grayson Perry's mouth
'is like saying that racism was in crisis in the American south'.)

But back to your question.
Well, daughters, I think there's more than one issue,
but as problems often are,
they're linked, threaded within masculinity's narrow definition.
But let's start with this – imagine yourself an alien,
new on the earth

and in one fluid glance you survey our world.
This, in numbers, is part of what you see, just here,
in this country.
90% of violent crime is committed by men.
75% of all crime, the same.
95% of prison inmates, men again.
98% of sexual offences are committed by men
45% of women have experienced domestic abuse,
sexual assault or stalking.
A man brought up in a house where such activity happens
is three to four times more likely to become an abuser himself.
In a survey in the U.S. where teenage girls and boys were asked,
which, of all their fears, was the greatest one,
the girls' most common answer was being raped,
assaulted or killed.
The boys? Being ridiculed, the subject of laughter.
So, Larkin, perhaps not just man passing on misery to man,
but also creating it for women.
And daughters, now I hope you can see, why with all the world
to reform,
I chose people like me.

You cast your alien eyes wide, across the globe.
Every example of systemic oppression you find is designed
and governed by men.
The reckless despoiling of the planet, that too is dominated by
them,
as, for that matter, is the doubting of the consequences of the
same.

Violent extremism of every religion Christian, Muslim – again –
overwhelmingly stoked, devised and crimes in its name
committed by men.
The greed-driven, overly risky financial models that crash
bringing austerity and ruin – Yep you guessed it –
the architects and cultures of these,
also rooted in traditional masculinity.

By now your alien jaw is on the floor. This is extraordinary.
To call a spade a spade, from what you can tell,
nearly all this planet's wrong
is done by 50% of the population, by the half that's male.
But then, you realise, at least the source is clear, and therefore
also the solution.
Surely, you think, opening up your single alien ear,
this must be the talk on everyone's lips.
'Look at all this harm that men have done,
but at least we now know it's done by them,
so hooray, we can roll up our sleeves and sort this thing.'

You listen. Nothing. A few whispers on the wind,
the odd lone voice
raising the cry, but on the whole the talk
around issues of identity seems to be about mostly others
instead.
Women, as we've already said, minorities, races, sexualities,
but men, in the shape of those who have shaped our world?
Nope, the figures are there, plain to see, as are they,
but the debate to tackle them, it's strangely empty.

You raise your alien eyebrows in surprise,
'maybe I've missed something' you surmise.
So you look again, but what you see just confuses you more.
Because this issue of men, it seems, is hurting them too,
whether rich or poor. Violence, for example, it's now clear to you,
is a male disease, but its victims are men as well
as their female partners, daughters, and wives.

In the UK, you learn, men are 80% of the victims of violent
attack, and 85% of those committing suicide –
and that, death by their own hand, is the single biggest killer
for males under 45.

You stop to take that in. Surely that if nothing else,
is a canary in the mine?

But it doesn't stop there, because men, you see,
despite undoubtedly reaping the advantages of a male-biased
system –
in wages, opportunities, power and authority –
are still, beyond violence, being hurt by masculinity.
80% of rough sleepers are men, for one,
or here's another – four times more likely, as boys,
to suffer with difficulties of behaviour or emotion,
and three times more likely to be excluded from school.
Then, on the more granular level that's harder to measure,
the way a constrained vision of masculinity
can be detrimental to their happiness and well-being,
and of course, their relationships with women.

Long hours in the office, short hours with the family,
increased loneliness, fewer close friends,
a decline in the jobs that once gave them identity.

What's odd, you notice, is that the social effects
of stereotyping on girls are well known, monitored and talked
about,
as they should be – eating disorders, sexual harassment,
career progressions cut short, domestic and wages inequality.
But the effects upon boys and men? A lack of close friendships,
sexist attitudes,
workplace stress, exposure to violence and poorer health –
relatively, these go under the radar of the stereotype effect.

In response, I'm sure some will say, hey this isn't all down
to the gender roles we project. And of course, there
are other factors too, but I still say the masculinity
we have now doesn't leave men well equipped
for when *that* version of manhood has failed for them.
Because think about it. You're raised to be dominant,
competitive,
the bread-winner and a winner in the workplace too. Yet also,
having put the emphasis on power, physical and earning,
and neglected emotional learning, when things go south,
so does the man – humiliated, unable to talk, retreating into the
reticence, risk and violence
that's always been part of their schooling.
The Samaritans again – 'marriage breakdown is much more
likely to lead to suicide for men than women'.

As Rebecca Asher says in her book *Man Up*,
'Men who are socially excluded, unqualified
and uncared for fare much worse than their female
counterparts.'

And for me, that goes to the matter's heart.
If the view of your gender you inherit
is narrow and built on myths from an age not yours,
when it doesn't work out and you're left with no power, status,
authority,
all of which you've been told is what makes you, you,
what do you fall back on? Options are what you need.
Another way to be, to navigate your recovery.
And for 'traditional man', as prescribed as he is, they're few.

So daughters, this alien you've been pretending to be,
they're off now, they've seen enough, they're not sticking around,
but before they go they take a global view of what all this might
cost.

Literally, in money, it's a lot. Male violence in the UK alone
costs around 30 billion a year. So, imagine that multiplied
across the continents and nations.

In lost lives and unlived potential, again as we've seen, the cost is
too much.
And what about the planet itself? The drivers of climate change
– aggressive resource extraction, profit-driven short-termism
and then, in response to the threat,
an oddly irrational inaction.

Would the same have happened under the eyes of more balanced
men?
Or if the reins of energy were in the hands of women?

Ok, the alien is off. Time to go.
But we, my children, we're still here.
We can't just observe then run.
I mean the boys of now and the future are the men you'll meet,
so I'm guessing you'd like something done?
All well and good Dad being so down on the state of men, but if
it's really so bad, and you're so smart, then what's your solution?

Good question.

*

Well, for starters, this. Have the conversation.
And not just the what –
how we talk about it, that in itself would be a great leap forward.
Be enquiring, ambitious, aware of what gender is and is doing,
for all.
And where we have it too.
In festivals, great, but also in the media, soaps, pubs, films and,
most importantly I'd say, in school classrooms and halls.
Maybe statutory lessons for boys and girls about
what's expected of them as men and women,
and why that's the case and should it be?
Let them discuss those stats I shared with you,
and see how they'd imagine a different way forward,
let them talk it through,

not just in terms of what's gone wrong, but also the benefits,
rewards.

As part of this conversation the groups already having it now,
like Great Men here in Great Britain, or Men Can Stop Rape
in the United States, should be supported by governments
to expand the work they do in taking alternative
visions of being a man to boys and young men.
Because new role models should be encouraged everywhere,
at home, in the media and in schools of course too.
Why not a quota or a target for men as teachers from infant
to secondary school? National programmes of male mentoring
and fostering? A concerted effort to put the shoulder
to the wheel to make a better man.

It's something that already happens, one-to-one.
When asked about a 'strong man' in their life,
it's interesting how many men describe not someone
of physical or commanding power, but rather
a man who's given them counsel, advice, offered compassion.
 Let's listen to that quiet message.

Which brings me to rites of passage.
Every culture, in every time, has had one for men,
a moment of transition where time is given
to thinking, and acting out, who you want to become.
So where is ours now? There are maybe two of a legal kind,
I'd say, both informal – sport and the army.
For some these can do the trick –
offer a sense of purpose, identity and most importantly,

belonging. But both are based in easy certainty – win, lose,
train, obey, and in all the fundamentals of 'trad' man too.
So what happens when they end? I've worked with men
conditioned by both, and seen how vulnerable they can be
when the physical, for whatever reason, fails.
Emotionally, these most 'manly' of men, can seem like children –
unschooled in the blurred lines of the world, unsure of how to be
or what to do, emerging from landscapes of sexism,
into a more complex world where, often, it's a woman in their
lives who pulls them through.

So what else might we do? To mark and reflect on that moment
of boy to man? I don't know exactly, but I know we have to –
provide a space for reflection and aspiration, to consider
the values we want to uphold and be. To ask how,
as well as a being a man, might I be me?

Here's another thing that has to happen.
Absolute equality, at home, work, across society.
Why? Well, if boys see and experience patriarchy,
if they observe an assumed male superiority,
then we can't even get out of the starting blocks.
Because this is part of the narrow bandwidth.
If men are dominant then with that comes
a shopping list of other constrictive traits – being the provider,
power, authority, sexism, a reliance on certainty, strength.
As the anthropologist, Margaret Mead once said –
'Every time we liberate a woman, we liberate a man'
and, I'd say, the opposite of that is true as well,
because if we do, hopefully, men will see there's nothing to fear.

Equality isn't, and shouldn't be, a zero sum game,
it's not a see-saw – when one goes up, the other goes down.
No, it's balance, holding that see-saw in buoyant space,
alive with possibility, not anchored at one end,
and suspended at the other.

'But what,' I hear you say, 'about us? The children?
When we come along men and women
become father and mother. Doesn't that put a spanner
in the equality works?'

Well yes, it always has done, but doesn't have to.
If we want a better society then it's in our power to shape it.
The ocean shelf slopes up as well, remember?
So, to start with, subsidized universal childcare, across the board
for all pre-school children. And paid, equal, parental leave.
Being involved as a Dad needs to become the norm –
the choice of who cares and how much,
made within each family, not by society.

For this to happen men need to be not just invited
to take their leave, adopt flexible hours, but also expected.
How does that happen? Well, apart from changing the culture
of work to adopt this, also in stressing the benefits.
I mean, it's a win-win situation – children experience
and see men in a caring role, while, and it's been proved
in the Nordic countries where this is already on the move,
men are happier, more socially connected, more emotionally
stable

if they feel they can exchange the stress from above
of putting food on the table, for caring for their children –
for providing for them not just with money,
but also time, emotion, love.

Some say this will be the hardest sell,
the most difficult thing to do. But I'm not so sure.
I've played rugby, ridden stallions in the hills, climbed
Kilimanjaro. But I've never felt more of a man,
or a human, than when being a father to you.

A couple of other equality points.
One – the concept needs backing in the courts.
Laws, like the new bill passed in Iceland that punishes
unequal pay.
Two – our governments should lead by example.
Set a female MP target of 50% in parliament.

Okay, I'm going to bring this to a close now
but before I go, a couple of more ambitious ideas.
I mean, what's the point of imagining reform
if you don't let yourself dream?

So here's one – the de-gendering of personality traits.
What would it be like if we stopped identifying aggression
with men, emotions and communication with women?
To allow boys and girls to grow up free of expectation
as to who their sex means they should be?
To organize their roles in life, in relationships, as they see fit?

To be people who are many things and types
and who share, perhaps, more than we think?
To do away with the idea of 'girl's jobs, and boy's jobs'
(thanks Mrs May) and say to our children,
follow your instincts, your wishes, your ideas,
free from prescription or boundaries or fears.

For the time being though, in terms of men,
how about we at least try expanding on the traits
we traditionally associate with them?
To protect and provide, for example.
What if we were to 'man up' on this one,
and extend our vision of what is provision,
protection, beyond our own tribe. To see it in
terms of our species instead? Until to do either
in such a way that somewhere else, someone else,
is left unprotected or unprovided, just isn't manly at all.
If we follow this logic then environmentalists, climate activists,
never usually spoken of in the most masculine terms,
should be the guyest guys of us all.
protecting the whole *planet* and in doing so,
trying to provide for *everyone*? Wow, now that's a man,
lifting his eyes from his own back door
to take in the globe, to protect and provide for us all.

What about bravery? We teach our boys to be physically brave –
why not emotionally too? And strength – is just physical enough
anymore,
or to survive in the modern world shouldn't a man
be strong in well-being, empathy, mental health too?

I could go on, but you get the gist. Expand the traits
of each gender until, well, they just meet,
and then what do you get? People, full of difference,
yes, but humans all the same, raising their game.

So, daughters, let's end on a vision
of what men and masculinity might be
by the time you're my age, 42, 43.

A person with chromosomes of X and Y,
for whom power without compassion is no power at all,
for whom strength has been de-coupled from domination.
For whom to be fit, healthy, means in body, mind and emotion.
For whom oppression is equated with fear in the oppressor,
aggression with failure on the part of the aggressor.
For whom the ability to be vulnerable makes him strong,
as does that to be unsure, uncertain, even wrong.
A male allowed to contain Whitman's multitudes,
who has cared for and witnessed the growth of his children
or who, if he has none, is still positively involved, as mentor,
teacher
with the next generation, because not to be, would be, well,
unmanly.

Who, actually, would no longer be familiar with that word,
but would, in its place have another, for whatever not
being a human might mean.

I know, I know, I dream. But as your father that's part of my job.
Every parent wants to pass on something better.
and so far we're not doing so great.
A property, Europe, a fair economy,
the climate, I see it all slipping out of your grip.
But if we could pass on this vision, or even just a taste of it
for you to later form, then that, that would be getting something
done –

to know one day you two might read this,
each with a man or a woman by your side who'll look on in
disbelief that it was ever necessary to give such a speech.
Who'll put their arms around you, as you put yours around
them, all of you, beyond your sex, your own person,
as you wonder how it was we could have been so mad,
shaking your heads as you walk away,
saying with a smile each to the other, 'silly old Dad.'

Owen Sheers is an author, poet and playwright. Winner of the 2018 Wilfred Owen Poetry award, he has published two collections of poetry, *The Blue Book* and *Skirrid Hill*, which won a Somerset Maugham Award. His debut prose work, *The Dust Diaries*, won the Welsh Book of the Year and was shortlisted for the Royal Society of Literature Ondaatje Prize. His first novel, *Resistance*, has been translated into 11 languages and adapted as a film. His most recent novel, *I Saw A Man*, was shortlisted for the Prix Femina Etranger and is currently being adapted for TV.

Owen's theatrical writing includes National Theatre of Wales' 72-hour site-specific production, *The Passion*; a play created with wounded service personnel, *The Two Worlds of Charlie F*, which toured the UK and Canada and won the Amnesty International Freedom of Expression Award; and NTW's *Mametz*. His verse drama *Pink Mist* won the Hay Festival Poetry Medal and the Wales Book of the Year and was produced for the stage by Bristol Old Vic. His BBC film-poem to mark the 50th anniversary of the Aberfan disaster, *The Green Hollow*, won three BAFTA Cymru awards and was nominated for BAFTA and Grierson awards. The book of the film has recently been published by Faber. His latest film-poem, *To Provide All People*, will be published and broadcast in June 2018 to mark the 70th anniversary of the NHS. His one-man play about the WWII poet Keith Douglas, *Unicorns, almost*, premiered in Hay-on-Wye in 2018.

A recipient of the St David Award for Culture, Owen's professional positions have included Writer in Residence at the Wordsworth Trust, Artist in Residence with the Welsh Rugby Union and a Dorothy and Lewis B. Cullman Fellowship at the New York Public Library. He is currently Professor in Creativity at Swansea University, chair of Wales PEN Cymru and a trustee and co-founder of the Black Mountains College project.

Recommended by Laura Bates

For young people

Laura Bates, *Girl Up* (Simon & Schuster UK, 2016)

James Dawson, *Being a Boy* (Hot Key Books, 2013)

Elena Favilli and Francesca Cavallo, *Goodnight Stories for Rebel Girls* (Particular Books, 2017)

Caitlin Moran, *How to be a Woman* (Ebury Press, 2012)

Chimamanda Ngozi Adichie, *We Should All Be Feminists* (Fourth Estate, 2014)

Victoria Pepe, *I Call Myself a Feminist* (Virago, 2015)

Robert Webb, *How Not To Be a Boy* (Canongate Books, 2017)

For parents and educators

Melissa Atkins Wardy, *Redefining Girly* (Chicago Review Press, 2014)

Peggy Orenstein, *Cinderella Ate My Daughter* (Harper Paperbacks, 2012)

Natasha Walter, *Living Dolls* (Virago, 2011)

Recommended by Owen Sheers

Rebecca Asher, *Man Up: Boys, Men and Breaking the Male Rules* (Harvill Secker, 2016)

Raewyn W Connell, *Masculinities* (Polity Press, 2005)

Lise Eliot, *Pink Brain, Blue Brain: How small differences grow into troublesome gaps – and what we can do about it* (Oneworld Publications, 2012)

Cordelia Fine, *Delusions of Gender: The Real Science Behind Sex Difference* (Icon Books, 2011)

Jan Morris, *Conundrum* (Faber & Faber, 2002)

Grayson Perry, *The Descent of Man* (Allen Lane, 2016)

Jack Urwin, *Man Up: Surviving Modern Masculinity* (Icon Books Ltd, 2016)

www.great-men.org
www.mencanstoprape.org